2017

Pocket Guide to Transportation

U.S. Department of Transportation
Bureau of Transportation Statistics

ACKNOWLEDGMENTS

U.S. Department of Transportation

Elaine L. Chao
Secretary

Bureau of Transportation Statistics

Patricia Hu
Director

Rolf Schmitt
Deputy Director

Produced under the direction of:

Michael J. Sprung
Director, Office of Transportation Analysis

Sonya Smith
Project Manager

William Moore
Editor

Alpha Wingfield
Visual Information Specialist

Major Contributors:
Mindy Liu
Long Nguyen

Contributors:
Steve Beningo
Matthew Chambers
Chester Ford
Justyna Goworowska
Sean Jahanmir
Demi Riley (Spatial Front)
Jie Zhang (Spatial Front)

ABOUT THE
POCKET GUIDE TO TRANSPORTATION

The BTS *Pocket Guide to Transportation* is a quick reference guide to significant transportation statistics. All the previous seven sections plus a new Major Trends section are included.

This year marks the 20th anniversary of the *Pocket Guide*, which now features an innovative smart phone app. Download now to access all the popular features of the classic Pocket Guide (available for iPhone and iPad on the iTunes Apple Store and for Android on the Google Play store).

BTS welcomes comments and suggestions for improving this product.

CONTENTS

Major Trends
Moving People: January 2000–July 2016

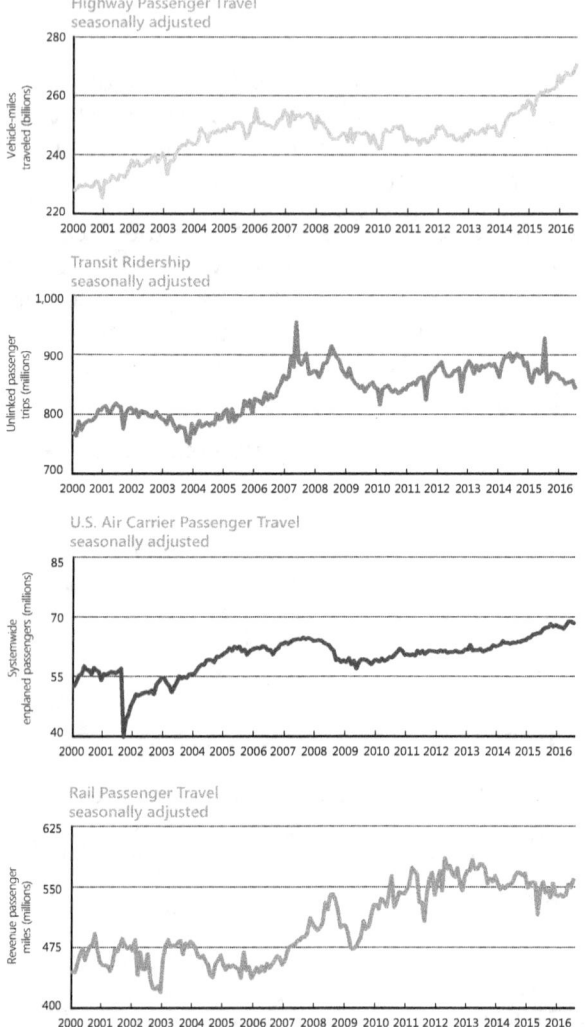

Notes: Graph scales are not comparable. Seasonally adjusted data measure the real differences in data trends by adjusting for seasonal factors, such as the change in the number of days, weekends, holidays, or other seasonal activity in a month such as vacation travel.

Source: Seasonally adjusted transportation data–U.S. Department of Transportation, Bureau of Transportation Statistics, available at www.bts.gov as of October 2016.

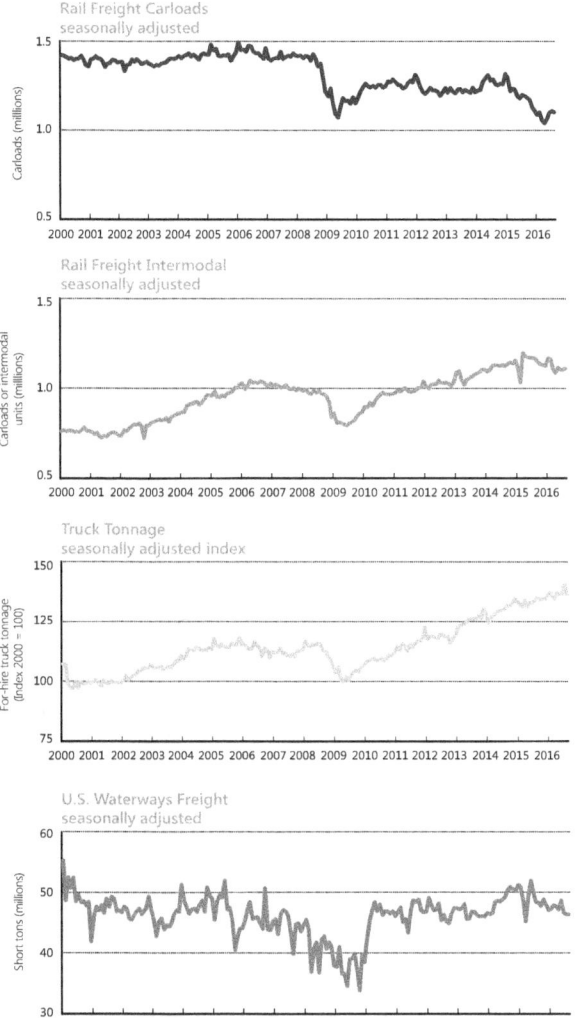

Notes: Graph scales are not comparable. **Rail Freight Intermodal**–Rail inter-modal traffic includes shipping containers and truck trailers moved on rail cars. **U.S. Waterways Freight**–Includes tonnage carried on internal U.S. waterways.

Source: Seasonally adjusted transportation data–U.S. Department of Transportation, Bureau of Transportation Statistics, available at www.bts.gov as of October 2016.

1   INFRASTRUCTURE

The U.S. transportation system consists of a network of roads, bridges, airports, railroads, transit systems, ports, waterways, and pipelines connecting the Nation to the rest of the world.

1-1   Transportation Network Length
miles

Mode	2004	2014
Highway		
Public roads	3,981,512	4,177,073
Public road lanes[a]	8,338,821	8,766,049
Pipeline		
Gas distribution	1,925,748	2,169,155
Gas transmission and gathering	327,994	319,313
Rail		
Class I freight railroad	97,662	94,372
Amtrak	22,256	21,356
Transit		
Commuter rail[b]	6,875	7,795
Heavy rail[b]	1,596	1,622
Light rail[b,c]	1,187	1,877
Water		
Navigable waterways[d]	25,000	25,000

[a]Measured in lane-miles. [b]Measured in directional route-miles. [c]Light rail was revised beginning in 2011 and includes light rail, street car rail, and hybrid rail. [d]Estimated length of domestic waterways.

Sources: Highway, Rail, Transit, Water–As cited in U.S. Department of Transportation, Bureau of Transportation Statistics, *National Transportation Statistics*, tables 1-1, 1-6, and 1-10, available at www.bts.gov as of October 2016. **Pipeline**–U.S. Department of Transportation, Pipeline and Hazardous Materials Administration, available at phmsa.dot.gov/pipeline/library/data-stats as of October 2016.

1-2　Transportation Facilities
number

Mode	2004	2014
Air		
Certificated airports[a]	599	537
General aviation airports	19,221	18,762
Highway		
Bridges	593,812	610,749
Pipeline		
LNG facilities	U	125
Rail		
Amtrak stations	529	518
Transit rail		
Commuter rail stations	1,163	1,245
Heavy rail stations	1,023	1,130
Light rail stations[b]	723	969
Water		
Ports[c]	191	183
Cargo handling docks[d]	*	8,229
Lock chambers	257	239

*2004 cargo handling docks number is omitted because it is not comparable to 2014 number due to a change in data collection methodology.

[a]Certificated airports serve air carrier operations with aircrafts seating more than nine passengers. [b]Light rail was revised beginning in 2011 and includes light rail, street car rail, and hybrid rail. [c]Ports handling over 250,000 short tons. [d]Data for 2004 and 2014 are not comparable due to changes in data coverage.

Key: LNG = liquified natural gas; U = Data are unavailable.

Sources: **Air, Highway, Rail**–As cited in U.S. Department of Transportation, Bureau of Transportation Statistics, *National Transportation Statistics*, tables 1-3, 1-7, and 1-28, available at www.bts.gov as of October 2016. **Pipeline**–U.S. Department of Transportation, Pipeline and Hazardous Materials Administration, available at phmsa.dot.gov/pipeline/library/data-stats as of October 2016. **Transit**–U.S. Department of Transportation, National Transit Database, available at www.ntdprogram.gov as of October 2016. **Water**–U.S. Army Corps of Engineers, Navigation Data Center, Transportation Facts and Information, available at www.navigationdatacenter.us as of October 2016.

1-3 Transportation Vehicles
number

Mode	2004	2014
Air		
Air carrier aircraft	7,764	6,676
General aviation aircraft	219,426	204,408
Highway		
Light-duty vehicle[a]	228,275,978	240,155,238
Truck	8,171,364	10,905,956
Motorcycle	5,767,934	8,417,718
Rail		
Class I freight locomotive	22,015	25,916
Class I freight car	473,773	371,642
Amtrak locomotive	276	428
Amtrak car	1,211	1,419
Transit rail		
Commuter rail[b]	6,130	7,177
Heavy rail[b]	10,858	10,551
Light rail[b, c]	1,622	2,444
Water		
Nonself-propelled vessel	31,296	31,043
Self-propelled vessel	8,994	9,039
Oceangoing vessel	233	179
Recreational boat	12,781,476	11,804,002

[a]Includes passenger cars, light trucks, vans, and sport utility vehicles. [b]Includes revenue vehicles available for maximum service. [c]Light rail was revised beginning in 2011.

Source: As cited in U.S. Department of Transportation, Bureau of Transportation Statistics, *National Transportation Statistics*, table 1-11, available at www.bts.gov as of September 2016.

1-4 Airport Runway Pavement Condition
percent of NPIAS runways

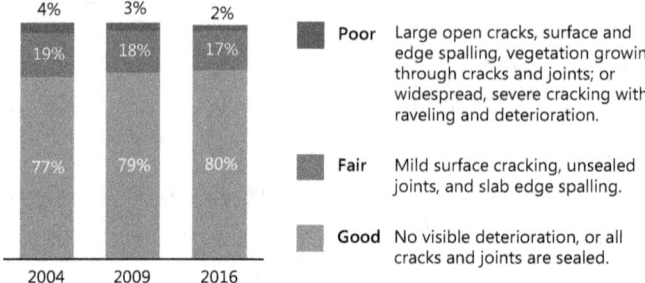

	Poor	Large open cracks, surface and edge spalling, vegetation growing through cracks and joints; or widespread, severe cracking with raveling and deterioration.
	Fair	Mild surface cracking, unsealed joints, and slab edge spalling.
	Good	No visible deterioration, or all cracks and joints are sealed.

Note: National Plan of Integrated Airport Systems (NPIAS) airports include commercial service airports, reliever airports, and selected general aviation airports.

Source: As cited in U.S. Department of Transportation, Bureau of Transportation Statistics, *National Transportation Statistics*, table 1-25, available at www.bts.gov as of October 2016.

1-5 National Highway System Pavement Condition
percent of NHS facility miles

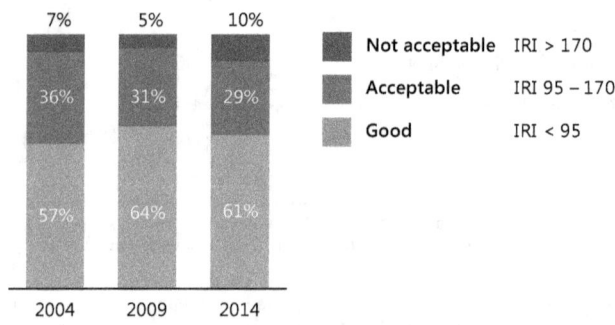

	Not acceptable	IRI > 170
	Acceptable	IRI 95 – 170
	Good	IRI < 95

Note: Pavement condition is measured by the International Roughness Index (IRI), which takes a longitudinal profile of pavement roughness based on centerline miles.

Source: U.S. Department of Transportation, Federal Highway Administration, Highway Statistics, table HM-47, available at https://www.fhwa.dot.gov/policyinformation/statistics.cfm as of October 2016.

1-6   Structurally Deficient Bridges: 1990–2015

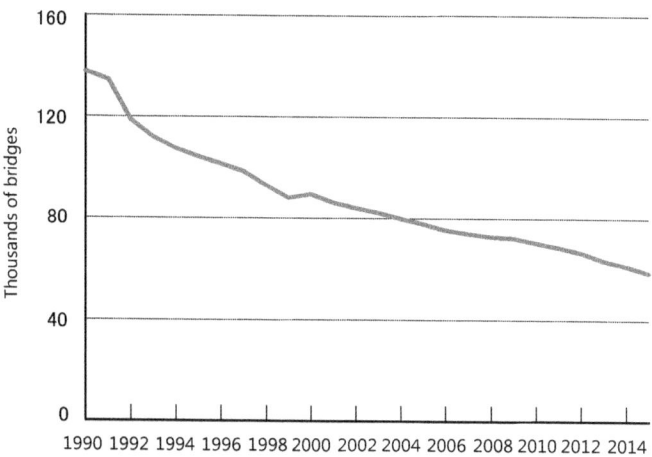

Source: As cited in U.S. Department of Transportation, Bureau of Transportation Statistics, *National Transportation Statistics*, tables 1-28, available at www.bts.gov as of October 2016.

1-7   Structurally Deficient Bridges by State: 2015

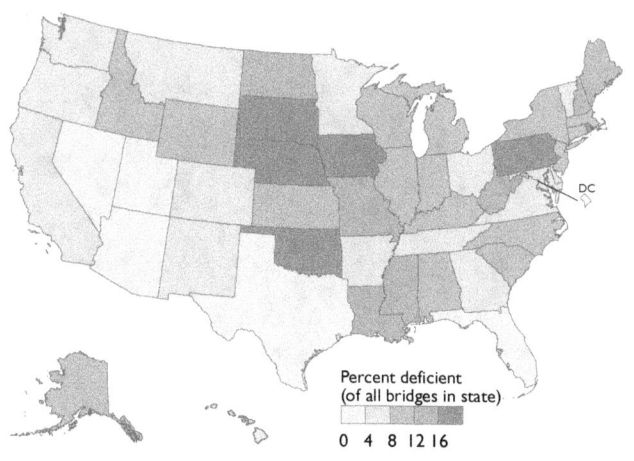

Source: U.S. Department of Transportation, Federal Highway Administration, National Bridge Inventory, available at www.fhwa.dot.gov/bridge/nbi.cfm as of October 2016.

Infrastructure 5

2   MOVING PEOPLE

The U.S. transportation system makes personal mobility possible. Every day people use the transportation system to get to and from work, school, and shopping and for recreation, social, and personal purposes.

2-1   Vehicle-Miles Traveled
millions

Mode	2007	2014
Air		
U.S. air carrier, domestic[a]	6,733	5,947
Highway		
Light-duty vehicle[b]	2,691,034	2,710,556
Motorcycle	21,396	19,970
Truck	304,178	279,132
Bus	14,516	15,999
Passenger rail		
Amtrak[c]	267	325
Commuter rail	325	367
Heavy rail[c]	657	676
Light rail[c, d]	84	114

[a]Measured in revenue aircraft-miles. [b]Includes passenger cars, light trucks, vans, and sport utility vehicles. [c]Measured in passenger car-miles. [d]Light rail was revised beginning in 2011 and includes light rail, street car rail, and hybrid rail

Note: Data for 2007 and later years may not be comparable to previous years due to changes in methodology.

Source: As cited in U.S. Department of Transportation, Bureau of Transportation Statistics, *National Transportation Statistics*, table 1-35, available at www.bts.gov as of October 2016.

2-2 Highway Travel: 1970–2014

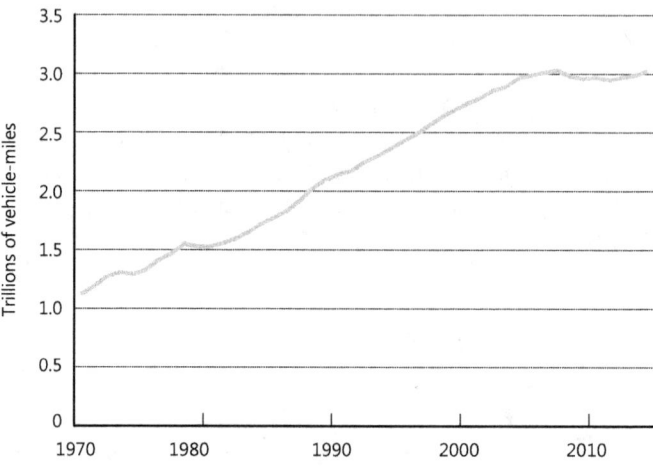

Note: Data for 2007 and later years may not be comparable to previous years due to changes in methodology.

Source: U.S. Department of Transportation, Federal Highway Administration, Highway Statistics, available at http://www.fhwa.dot.gov/policyinformation/ statistics.cfm as of October 2016.

2-3 Passenger-Miles Traveled

millions

Mode	2007	2014
Air		
U.S. air carrier, domestic	607,564	607,772
Highway		
Light-duty vehicle[a]	4,341,984	3,731,888
Motorcycle	27,173	21,510
Truck	304,178	279,132
Bus	307,753	339,177
Passenger rail		
Amtrak[b]	5,784	6,675
Commuter rail	11,137	11,600
Heavy rail	16,138	18,339
Light rail[c]	1,930	2,675

[a]Includes passenger cars, light trucks, vans, and sport utility vehicles.
[b]Measured in revenue passenger-miles. [c]Light rail was revised beginning in 2011 and includes light rail, street car rail, and hybrid rail.

Note: Data for 2007 and later years may not be comparable to previous years due to changes in methodology.

Source: As cited in U.S. Department of Transportation, Bureau of Transportation Statistics, *National Transportation Statistics*, table 1-40, available at www.bts.gov as of October 2016.

2-4 Transit Ridership: 1970–2014

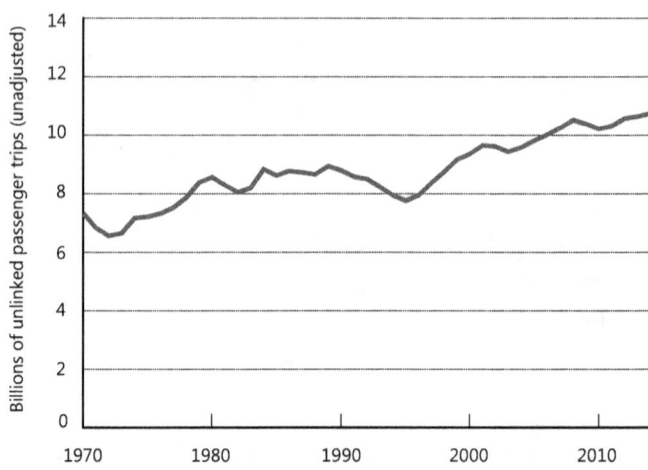

Note: Includes bus, commuter rail, demand response, heavy rail, light rail, trolley bus, ferry boat, aerial tramway, automated guideway, cable car, inclined plane, monorail, and other.

Source: American Public Transportation Association, *Public Transportation Fact Book*, National Transit Database (Appendix), available at www.apta.com as of October 2016.

2-5 Daily Passenger Travel

	1995	2001	2009
Travel per person			
Daily person trips	4.3	3.7	3.8
Daily person-miles	38.7	36.9	36.1
Travel per driver			
Daily vehicle trips	3.6	3.4	3.0
Daily vehicle-miles of travel	32.1	32.7	29.0
Average commute			
Length in miles	11.6	12.1	11.8
Travel time in minutes	20.7	23.3	23.9
Percent of trips by mode			
Private vehicle	89.3	86.4	83.4
Bus[a]	3.0	2.8	3.3
Rail[b]	0.6	0.6	0.6
Walk	5.5	8.7	10.4
Bike	0.9	0.8	1.0
Air	0.1	0.1	0.1
Other[c]	0.5	0.6	1.1

[a]Includes local transit bus, commuter bus, school bus, charter/tour bus, city-to-city bus. [b]Includes subway/elevated rail, street car/trolley, Amtrak/intercity train, and commuter train. [c]Includes ferry, hotel/airport shuttle, light electric vehicle, limousine, passenger line/ferry, sailboat/motorboat/yacht, ship/cruise, special transit, taxicab, other, and unknown.

Note: Percents may not add to 100 due to rounding.

Source: U.S. Department of Transportation, Federal Highway Administration, *2009 National Household Travel Survey*, available at nhts.ornl.gov as of October 2016.

2-6 Commute Mode Share: 2015

percent of workers age 16 and older

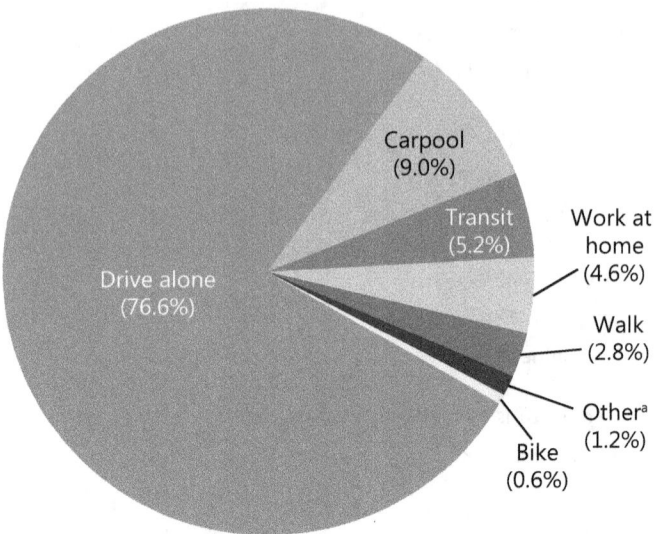

Carpool
(9.0%)

Transit
(5.2%)

Work at
home
(4.6%)

Drive alone
(76.6%)

Walk
(2.8%)

Other[a]
(1.2%)

Bike
(0.6%)

[a] Includes motorcycle, taxi, and other means.

Notes: Percents may not add to 100 due to rounding. The *American Community Survey* asks for the mode usually used by the respondent to get to work. For more than one mode of transportation, respondents select the mode used for most of the distance traveled.

Source: As cited in U.S. Department of Transportation, Bureau of Transportation Statistics, *National Transportation Statistics*, table 1-41, available at www.bts.gov as of October 2016.

2-7 Amtrak Ridership: FY2000–FY2015

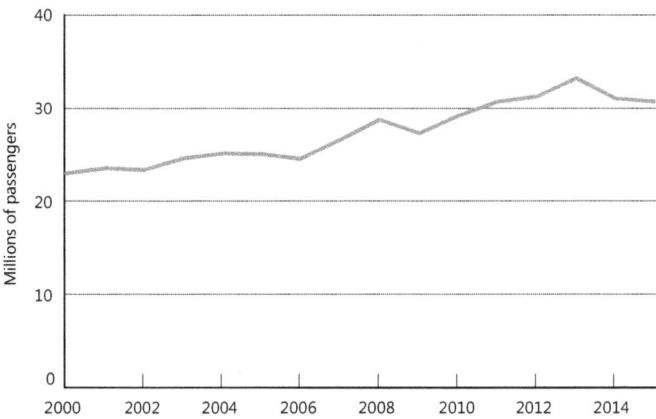

Source: U.S. Department of Transportation, Federal Railroad Administration, available at safetydata.fra.dot.gov/OfficeofSafety as of October 2016.

2-8 Top 10 Amtrak Stations: FY2015
by passengers

Rank	Station	FY '14–FY '15 change	Millions of passengers
1	New York Penn Station, NY	▲ 1.6%	10.2
2	Washington, DC	▼ -1.1%	5.0
3	Philadelphia 30th St., PA	▲ 1.3%	4.1
4	Chicago, IL	▼ -2.4%	3.3
5	Los Angeles, CA	▲ 2.5%	1.6
6	Boston South Station, MA	▲ 3.6%	1.5
7	Sacramento, CA	▲ 0.5%	1.0
8	Baltimore, MD	▼ -3.8%	1.0
9	Albany-Rensselaer, NY	▲ 5.6%	0.8
10	San Diego, CA	▲ 10.5%	0.8

Note: Includes passenger boardings and alightings.

Source: Amtrak, *National Fact Sheet and State Fact Sheet*, available at www.amtrak.com as of October 2016.

2-9 U.S. Air Carrier Passenger Traffic: 2003–2015

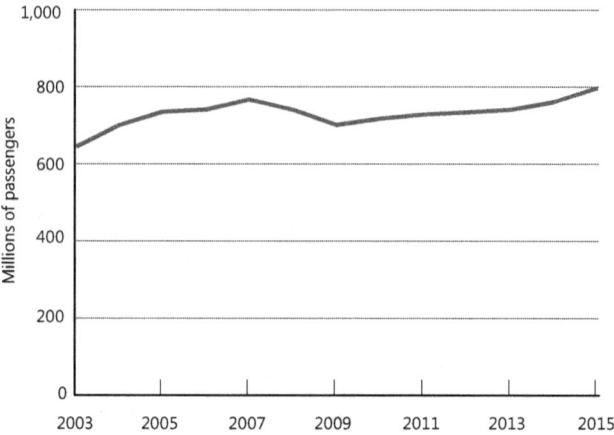

Note: Includes passenger enplanements on scheduled services only (domestic and international flights).

Source: U.S. Department of Transportation, Bureau of Transportation Statistics, Office of Airline Information, T-100 Market data, available at www.bts.gov as of October 2016.

2-10 Top 10 U.S. Airports: 2015
by enplaned passengers

Rank	Station	'14-'15 change	Millions of passengers
1	Atlanta, GA	6.1%	49.8
2	Los Angeles, CA	6.0%	37.1
3	Chicago O'Hare, IL	7.5%	36.5
4	Dallas/Fort Worth, TX	2.7%	31.7
5	New York JFK, NY	6.4%	28.0
6	Denver, CO	0.8%	26.6
7	San Francisco, CA	6.5%	24.4
8	Charlotte, NC	1.3%	22.2
9	Las Vegas, NV	5.8%	22.1
10	Phoenix, AZ	4.5%	21.9

Note: Includes passenger enplanements on U.S. carrier scheduled domestic and international service and foreign carrier scheduled international service to and from the United States.

Source: As cited in U.S. Department of Transportation, Bureau of Transportation Statistics, *National Transportation Statistics*, table 1-44, available at www.bts.gov as of October 2016.

2-11 Top 10 World Airports: 2015

by enplaned, deplaned, and in-transit passengers

Rank	Airport	'14-'15 change	Millions of passengers	
1	Atlanta, USA	5.5%		101.5
2	Beijing, China	4.4%		89.9
3	Dubai, United Arab Emirates	10.7%		78.0
4	Chicago, USA	9.9%		76.9
5	Tokyo, Japan	3.4%		75.3
6	London, United Kingdom	2.2%		75.0
7	Los Angeles, USA	6.0%		74.9
8	Hong Kong, China	8.2%		68.3
9	Paris, France	3.1%		65.8
10	Dallas/Fort Worth, USA	0.8%		64.1

Note: Preliminary data for passengers enplaned, deplaned, and passengers in transit.

Source: Airports Council International, available at www.aci.aero as of October 2016.

2-12 Incoming Land Border Person Crossings: 1995–2015

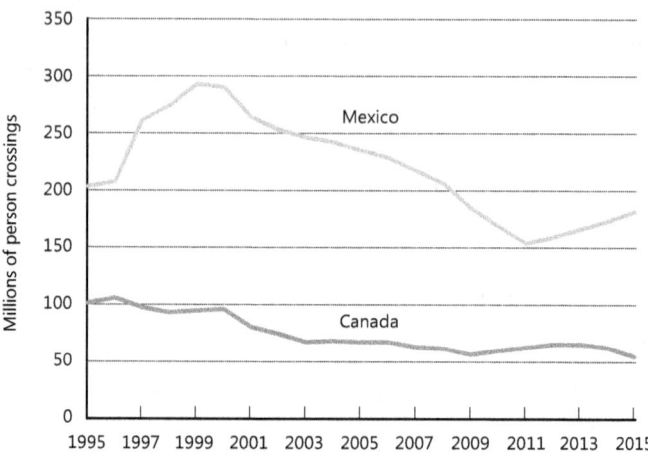

Note: Excludes drivers and passengers in commercial trucks.

Source: U.S. Department of Transportation, Bureau of Transportation Statistics, Border Crossing/Entry Data, available at www.bts.gov as of October 2016.

U.S. - Mexico ports of entry

Rank	Port	'14-'15 change	Millions of person crossings
1	San Ysidro, CA	12.2%	33.1
2	El Paso, TX	4.1%	27.1
3	Otay Mesa, CA	0.8%	15.8
4	Laredo, TX	4.7%	15.5
5	Hidalgo, TX	1.3%	12.0

U.S. - Canada ports of entry

Rank	Port	'14-'15 change	Millions of person crossings
1	Buffalo-Niagara Falls, NY	▼ -9.3%	11.3
2	Blaine, WA	▼ -15.4%	8.5
3	Detroit, MI	▼ -2.3%	7.2
4	Port Huron, MI	▼ -16.7%	3.3
5	Champlain-Rouses Pt., NY	▼ -9.2%	2.7

Note: Excludes drivers and passengers in commercial trucks.

Source: U.S. Department of Transportation, Bureau of Transportation Statistics, Border Crossing/Entry Data, available at www.bts.gov as of October 2016.

3 MOVING GOODS

The freight transportation network links natural resources, manufacturing facilities, labor markets, and customers across the Nation and with international trading partners.

3-1 Freight Shipments Within the U.S. by Mode

Value of shipments (billions of chained 2012 dollars)

Mode	2012	2015	2045
Truck	12,403	13,267	24,455
Rail	756	842	1,823
Water	433	500	885
Air and truck-air	672	794	3,240
Pipeline	1,301	1,462	1,817
Multiple modes[a]	1,979	2,131	4,341
Other[b]	259	262	520
Total	**17,803**	**19,258**	**37,081**

Weight of shipments (millions of tons)

Mode	2012	2015	2045
Truck	10,781	11,513	16,543
Rail	1,820	1,788	2,295
Water	654	729	946
Air and truck-air	7	7	24
Pipeline	2,932	3,315	4,563
Multiple modes[a]	383	398	646
Other[b]	376	306	328
Total	**16,953**	**18,056**	**25,345**

[a]Includes mail. [b]Includes other, unknown, and imported crude oil with no domestic mode.

Notes: Details may not add to totals due to rounding. Includes domestic trade and the domestic portion of imports and exports.

Source: U.S. Department of Transportation, Bureau of Transportation Statistics and Federal Highway Administration, Freight Analysis Framework, Version 4.2, available at www.bts.gov as of October 2016.

3-2   U.S. Trade by Coasts and Borders: 1990–2015

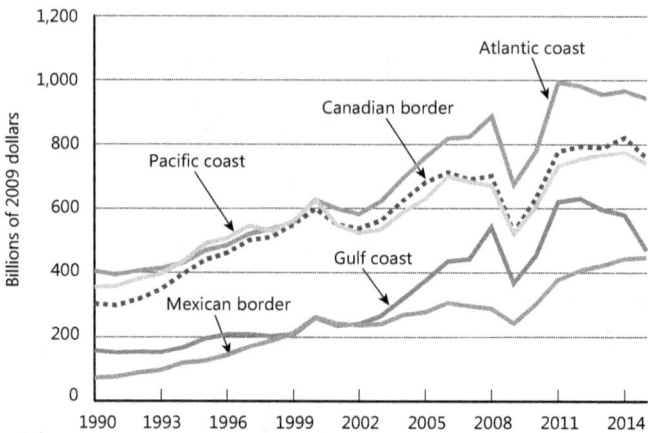

Note: Includes merchandise trade only.

Sources: **Value**–U.S. Department of Commerce, U.S. Census Bureau, Foreign Trade Division, available at www.census.gov as of June 2015. **Implicit GDP Deflator**– U.S. Department of Commerce, Bureau of Economic Analysis, available at www.bea.gov as of April 2016.

3-3 U.S.-NAFTA Merchandise Freight Trade by Mode: 2015

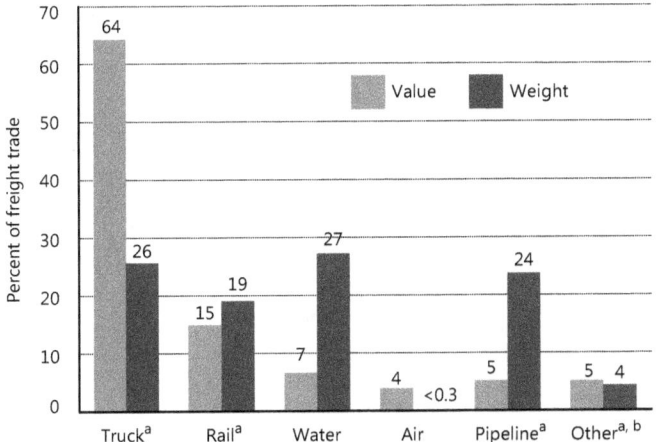

[a]Export weights for land modes are estimated by the Bureau of Transportation Statistics using value-to-weight ratios derived from import data. [b]Includes mail, other, unknown, and shipments through Foreign Trade Zones.

Notes: Percents do not add to 100 due to rounding. North American Free Trade Agreement (NAFTA) refers to U.S. trade with Canada and Mexico.

Source: U.S. Department of Transportation, Bureau of Transportation Statistics, special tabulation and North American Transborder Freight Data, available at www.bts.gov as of October 2016.

3-4 Incoming Truck Border Crossings: 1995–2015

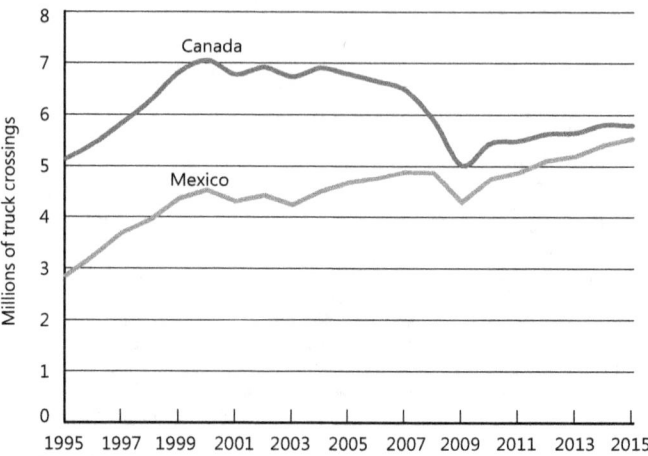

Source: As cited in U.S. Department of Transportation, Bureau of Transportation Statistics, *National Transportation Statistics*, table 1-53 and 1-55, available at www.bts.gov.as of October 2016.

U.S. - Canada ports of entry

Rank	Port	'14-'15 change	Millions of truck crossings
1	Detroit, MI	▼ -0.6%	1.5
2	Buffalo-Niagara Falls, NY	▼ -1.5%	0.9
3	Port Huron, MI	▲ 3.0%	0.8
4	Blaine, WA	▲ 2.9%	0.4
5	Champlain-Rouses Pt., NY	▲ 6.2%	0.3

U.S. - Mexico ports of entry

Rank	Port	'14-'15 change	Millions of truck crossings
1	Laredo, TX	▲ 3.5%	2.0
2	Otay Mesa, CA	▲ 2.4%	0.8
3	El Paso, TX	▼ -1.5%	0.7
4	Hidalgo, TX	▲ 3.0%	0.5
5	Calexico East, CA	▲ 3.8%	0.3

Source: As cited in U.S. Department of Transportation, Bureau of Transportation Statistics, *National Transportation Statistics*, tables 1-53 and 1-55, available at www.bts.gov.as of October 2016.

3-6 Top 10 U.S. Water Ports: 2014
by short tons

Rank	Port	'13-'14 change	Millions of short tons
1	South Louisiana	▲ 12.1%	267.4
2	Houston, TX	▲ 2.2%	234.3
3	New York/New Jersey	▲ 2.3%	126.2
4	Beaumont, TX	▼ -7.5%	87.3
5	Long Beach, CA	▲ 0.6%	85.0
6	Corpus Christi, TX	▲ 11.5%	84.9
7	New Orleans, LA	▲ 9.5%	84.5
8	Baton Rouge, LA	▲ 8.3%	69.2
9	Mobile, AL	▲ 19.1%	64.3
10	Los Angeles, CA	▲ 5.3%	61.0

by container TEUs, excluding foreign empty TEUs

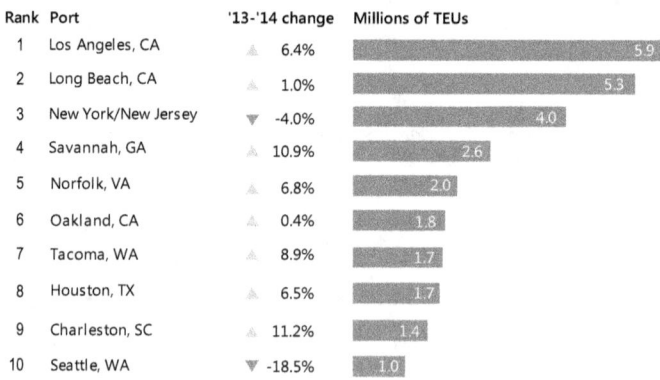

Rank	Port	'13-'14 change	Millions of TEUs
1	Los Angeles, CA	▲ 6.4%	5.9
2	Long Beach, CA	▲ 1.0%	5.3
3	New York/New Jersey	▼ -4.0%	4.0
4	Savannah, GA	▲ 10.9%	2.6
5	Norfolk, VA	▲ 6.8%	2.0
6	Oakland, CA	▲ 0.4%	1.8
7	Tacoma, WA	▲ 8.9%	1.7
8	Houston, TX	▲ 6.5%	1.7
9	Charleston, SC	▲ 11.2%	1.4
10	Seattle, WA	▼ -18.5%	1.0

Key: TEU = twenty-foot equivalent unit.

Note: Includes domestic and foreign waterborne trade.

Source: **Short tons** - As cited in U.S. Department of Transportation, Bureau of Transportation Statistics, *National Transportation Statistics*, table 1-57, available at www.bts.gov.as of October 2016. **Containers** - U.S. Army Corps of Engineers, Waterborne Commerce Statistics Center, available at www.navigationdatacenter.us as of October 2016.

3-7 Top 10 World Container Ports: 2014
by TEUs, including full and empty containers

Rank	Port	'13-'14 change	Millions of TEUs
1	Shanghai	5.0%	35.3
2	Singapore	4.0%	33.9
3	Shenzhen	2.2%	23.8
4	Hong Kong	0.1%	22.4
5	Ningbo	12.3%	19.5
6	Busan	4.6%	18.4
7	Quindao	7.1%	16.6
8	Guangzhou	5.6%	16.2
9	Dubai Ports	8.5%	14.8
10	Tianjin	8.1%	14.1
16	Los Angeles	6.0%	8.3
20	Long Beach	1.3%	6.8
24	New York/ New Jersey	5.6%	5.8

Key: TEU = twenty-foot equivalent unit.

Source: American Association of Port Authorities, *World Port Rankings*, available at www.aapa-ports.org as of October 2016.

3-8 Top 10 International Trade Gateways: 2015
by value of shipments

Rank	Port		'14-'15 change	Billions of dollars
1	New York/New Jersey, NY	⛴	▼ -1.9%	202.6
2	Los Angeles, CA	⛴	▼ -7.8%	198.4
3	Laredo, TX	🚚	▲ 2.7%	197.2
4	New York JFK Airport, NY	✈	▼ -3.2%	185.5
5	Long Beach, CA	⛴	▼ -12.8%	154.2
6	Chicago, IL	⛴	▲ 5.6%	141.8
7	Houston, TX	✈	▼ -18.4%	134.6
8	Detroit, MI	🚚	▼ -3.1%	128.9
9	Los Angeles Airport, CA	✈	▲ 8.2%	99.9
10	Savannah, GA	⛴	▲ 8.4%	87.3

Key:  ✈ = airport, 🚚 = land port, ⛴ = water port

Notes: Air gateways include a low level (generally less than 3% of the total value) of freight shipped through small user-fee airports located in the same area as the gateways listed. Air gateways not identified by airport name (e.g., Chicago, IL) include major airport(s) in the area and small regional airports.

Source: As cited in U.S. Department of Transportation, Bureau of Transportation Statistics, *National Transportation Statistics*, table 1-51, available at www.bts.gov as of October 2016.

4   SAFETY

Transportation safety is the top priority of the U.S. Department of Transportation.

4-1   Transportation Fatalities by Mode

Mode	2004	2014	2015
Air	637	444	404
U.S. air carrier	14	0	0
Commuter carrier	0	0	1
On-demand air taxi	64	20	27
General aviation	559	424	376
Highway	42,836	32,744	35,092
Passenger car occupants	19,192	11,947	12,628
Motorcyclists	4,028	4,594	4,976
Light-truck occupants	12,674	9,103	9,813
Heavy-truck occupants	766	656	667
Bus occupants	42	44	49
Pedestrians	4,675	4,910	5,376
Pedalcyclists	727	729	818
Other	732	761	765
Pipeline	23	19	10
Rail	891	767	759
Train accidents	13	5	13
Highway-rail grade crossing[a]	371	262	235
Trespassers	472	470	459
Other	35	30	52
Transit[a,b]	177	236	254
Water	815	674	692
Freight vessel and Industrial/Other	84	50	52
Passenger vessel and Recreational boating	731	624	640

[a] Individual modes don't add up to totals due to double counting in highway, rail, and transit grade crossings. [b] Includes transit employee, contract worker, passenger, revenue facility occupant, and other fatalities for all modes reported to the National Transit Database.

Source: As cited in U.S. Department of Transportation, Bureau of Transportation Statistics, *National Transportation Statistics*, table 2-1, available at www.bts. gov as of November 2016.

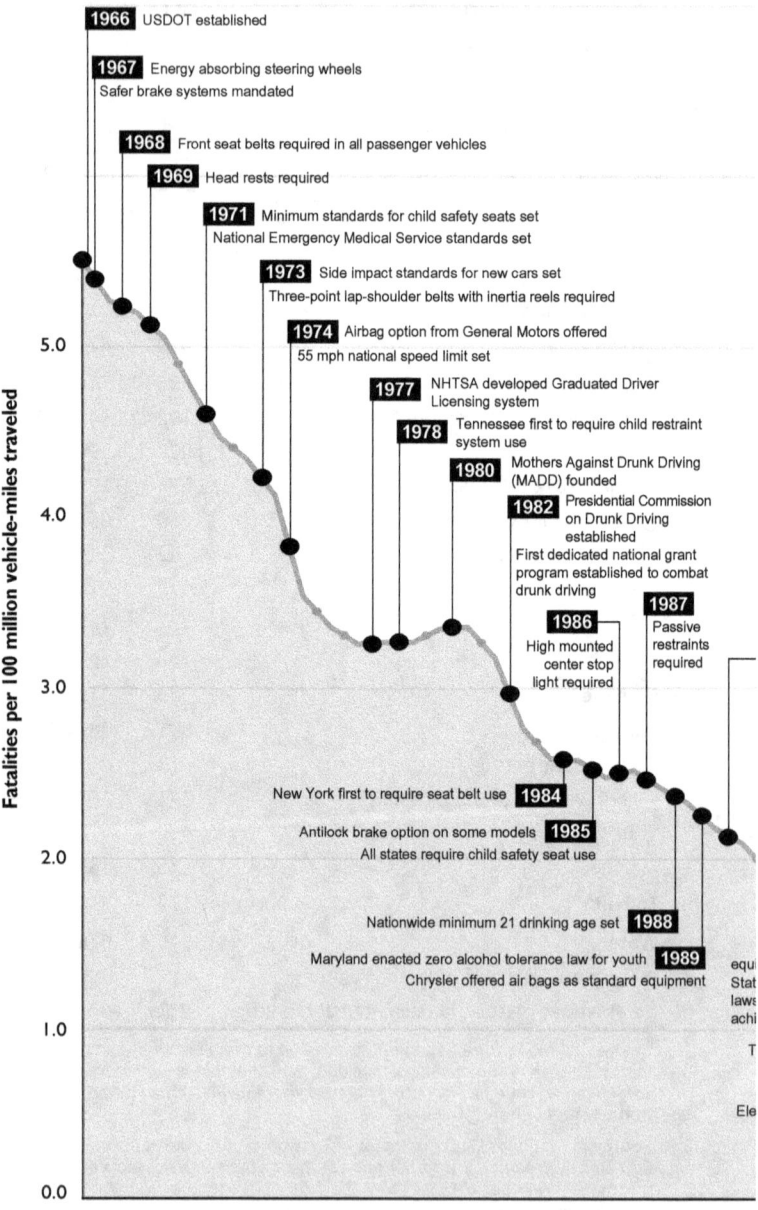

1966 USDOT established

1967 Energy absorbing steering wheels
Safer brake systems mandated

1968 Front seat belts required in all passenger vehicles

1969 Head rests required

1971 Minimum standards for child safety seats set
National Emergency Medical Service standards set

1973 Side impact standards for new cars set
Three-point lap-shoulder belts with inertia reels required

1974 Airbag option from General Motors offered
55 mph national speed limit set

1977 NHTSA developed Graduated Driver
Licensing system

1978 Tennessee first to require child restraint
system use

1980 Mothers Against Drunk Driving
(MADD) founded

1982 Presidential Commission
on Drunk Driving
established
First dedicated national grant
program established to combat
drunk driving

1987
Passive
restraints
required

1986
High mounted
center stop
light required

New York first to require seat belt use **1984**

Antilock brake option on some models **1985**
All states require child safety seat use

Nationwide minimum 21 drinking age set **1988**

Maryland enacted zero alcohol tolerance law for youth **1989**
Chrysler offered air bags as standard equipment

equi
Stat
laws
achi

T

Ele

Fatalities per 100 million vehicle-miles traveled

5.0

4.0

3.0

2.0

1.0

0.0

Final fatality data for 2016 are not available. Fatalities per 100 million vehicle-mil

Transportation safety is the top priority of the U.S. Department of Transportation. Although the cumulative effect of highway safety innovations coincides with a dramatic drop in highway fatalities, as seen in the timeline, a recent uptick in highway deaths and the highway death rate is a troubling development. The exact causes of these increases and what steps are needed to counter them are unclear.

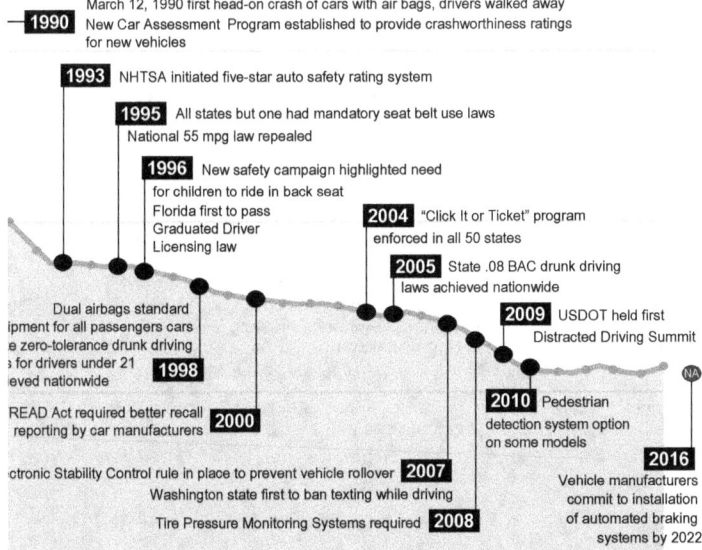

1990 March 12, 1990 first head-on crash of cars with air bags, drivers walked away
New Car Assessment Program established to provide crashworthiness ratings for new vehicles

1993 NHTSA initiated five-star auto safety rating system

1995 All states but one had mandatory seat belt use laws
National 55 mpg law repealed

1996 New safety campaign highlighted need for children to ride in back seat
Florida first to pass Graduated Driver Licensing law

2004 "Click It or Ticket" program enforced in all 50 states

2005 State .08 BAC drunk driving laws achieved nationwide

Dual airbags standard ipment for all passengers cars e zero-tolerance drunk driving s for drivers under 21 eved nationwide **1998**

2009 USDOT held first Distracted Driving Summit

READ Act required better recall reporting by car manufacturers **2000**

2010 Pedestrian detection system option on some models

ctronic Stability Control rule in place to prevent vehicle rollover **2007**
Washington state first to ban texting while driving
Tire Pressure Monitoring Systems required **2008**

2016 Vehicle manufacturers commit to installation of automated braking systems by 2022

es traveled climbed from 1.08 in 2014 to 1.12 in 2015 as fatalities increased 7.2 percent.

4-2 Transportation Injuries by Mode

Mode	2004	2014	2015
Air	297	262	282
U.S. air carrier	15	13	21
Commuter carrier	0	0	4
On-demand air taxi	17	15	9
General aviation	265	234	248
Highway	2,788,378	2,332,000	2,424,000
Passenger car occupants	1,642,549	1,292,000	1,378,000
Motorcyclists	76,379	92,000	88,000
Light-truck occupants	900,171	782,000	803,000
Heavy-truck occupants	27,287	27,000	30,000
Bus occupants	16,410	14,000	U
Pedestrians	67,985	65,000	70,000
Pedalcyclists	41,086	50,000	45,000
Other	16,511	10,000	10,000
Pipeline	56	93	49
Rail	9,194	8,731	8,962
Train Accidents	346	137	547
Highway-rail grade crossing[a]	1,094	870	1,023
Trespassers	406	422	414
Other	7,348	7,302	6,978
Transit[b]	20,478	24,045	24,252
Water	3,974	3,384	3,231
Freight vessel and Industrial/ Other	389	369	239
Passenger vessel and Recreational boating	3,585	3,015	2,992

[a]Excludes injuries involving motor vehicles at public highway-rail grade crossings, which are assumed to be counted under *Highway* categories. [b]Includes transit employee, contract worker, passenger, revenue facility occupant, and other injuries for all modes reported to the National Transit Database. Other transit injuries are assumed to be counted under *Highway* or *Rail* categories.

Source: As cited in U.S. Department of Transportation, Bureau of Transportation Statistics, *National Transportation Statistics*, table 2-2, available at www.bts.gov as of November 2016.

4-3 Fatality Rates by Mode

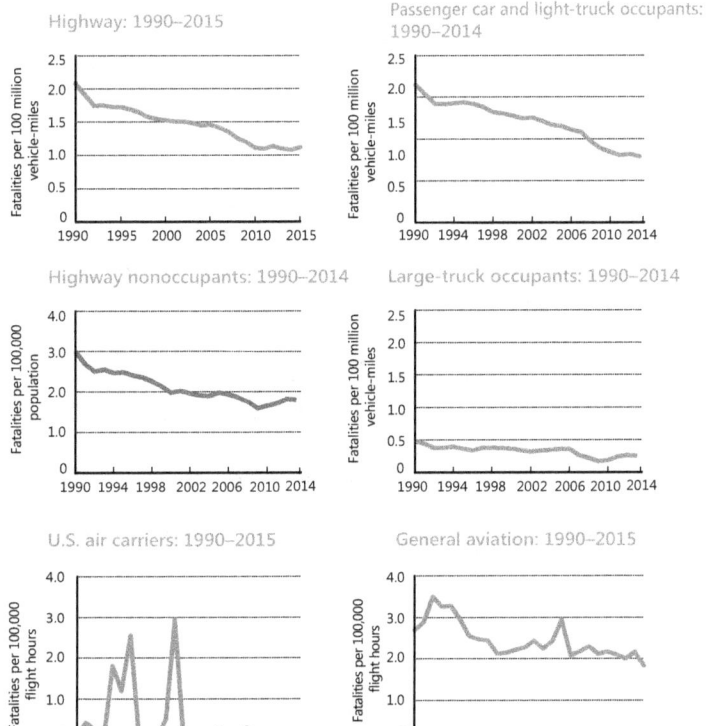

Highway: 1990–2015

Passenger car and light-truck occupants: 1990–2014

Highway nonoccupants: 1990–2014

Large-truck occupants: 1990–2014

U.S. air carriers: 1990–2015

General aviation: 1990–2015

Notes: Graphs with same color trend lines have identical scales. Air carrier fatalities resulting from the Sept. 11, 2001 terrorist acts include only onboard fatalities. Highway non-occupants include pedestrian, pedalcyclist, and other.

Sources: As cited in or calculated from U.S. Department of Transportation, Bureau of Transportation Statistics, *National Transportation Statistics*, tables 2-9, 2-14, 2-17, 2-19, 2-21, 2-23, and 3-10 available at www.bts.gov as of November 2016.

4-4 Alcohol-Impaired Driving Fatalities: 1990–2014

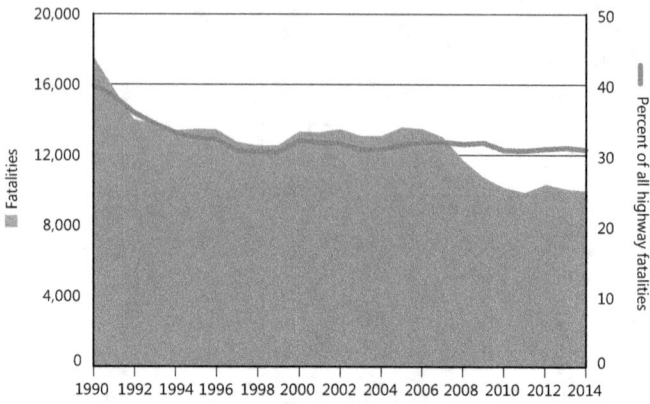

Note: Includes fatalities occurring in any crash involving a driver with a blood alcohol concentration (BAC) of 0.08 grams per deciliter or higher.

Source: U.S. Department of Transportation (USDOT), National Highway Traffic Safety Administration, Traffic Safety Facts: Alcohol-Impaired Driving (Annual Issues) as of November 2016.

4-5 Pedestrian and Bicyclist Fatalities: 1990–2015

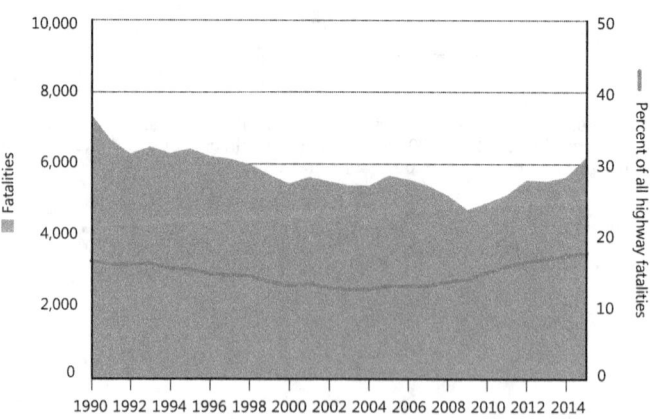

Note: Includes pedestrians and riders of nonmotorized bicycles and other pedal-powered vehicles.

Source: As cited in U.S. Department of Transportation, Bureau of Transportation Statistics, *National Transportation Statistics*, table 2-1, available at www.bts.gov as of November 2016.

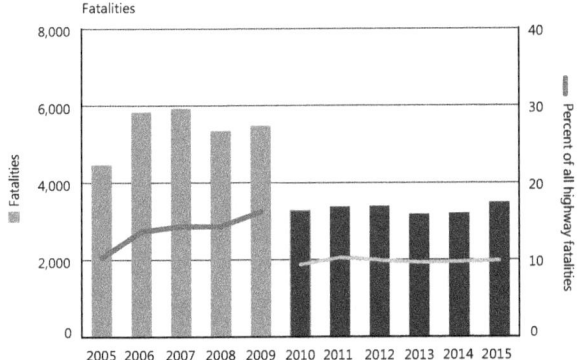

Fatalities

Note: Distracted driving fatality data for 2010 and on are not comparable with previous years due to changes in methodology.

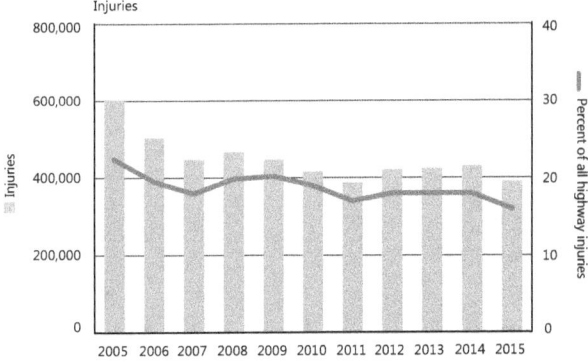

Injuries

Note: Distracted driving involves any activity that could divert a person's attention away from the primary task of driving, such as texting, using a cell phone, eating and drinking, grooming, using a navigation system, adjusting a radio, etc.

Source: U.S. Department of Transportation, National Highway Traffic Safety Administration, available at www.nhtsa.gov as of November 2016.

5 PERFORMANCE

The physical capacity of the U.S. transportation system has not kept pace with growth in travel and commerce. The resulting congestion and delays have significant impacts on passengers and freight shippers.

5-1 Road Congestion: 1985–2014

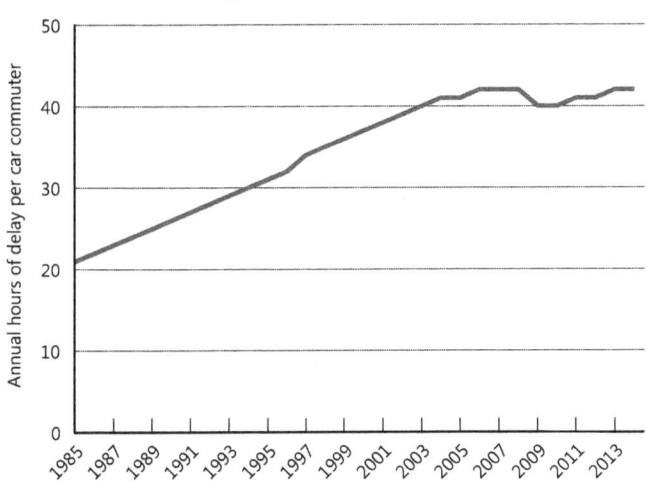

Notes: The methodology to calculate congestion performance measures was updated to reflect more comprehensive data collection, including congestion estimates for each of the 471 U.S. urban areas. The congestion estimates for all study years are recalculated every time the methodology is altered to provide a consistent data trend. For a detailed explanation of the updated methodology, see the 2015 Urban Mobility Scorecard Methodology, available at http://mobility.tamu.edu/ums/report/.

Source: As cited in U.S. Department of Transportation, Bureau of Transportation Statistics, *National Transportation Statistics*, table 1-69, available at www.bts.gov as of October 2016.

5-2 Top 10 Urban Congested Area Rankings: 2014
by hours of delay per car commuter

Rank	Urban area	Annual hours of delay per car commuter
1	Washington, DC-VA-MD	82
2	Los Angeles, CA	80
3	San Francisco, CA	78
4	New York, NY-NJ	74
5	Boston, MA-NH-RI	64
6	Seattle, WA	63
7	Chicago, IL-IN	61
7	Houston, TX	61
9	Dallas-Fort Worth-Arlington, TX	53
10	Atlanta, GA	52
	Average of 471 urban areas	42

Notes: Ranks include very large geographic areas only. The methodology was updated to reflect more comprehensive data collection efforts for each of the 471 U.S. urban areas.

Source: As cited in U.S. Department of Transportation, Bureau of Transportation Statistics, *National Transportation Statistics*, table 1-69, available at www.bts.gov as of October 2016.

5-3   U.S. Airport On-Time Performance: 1995–2015

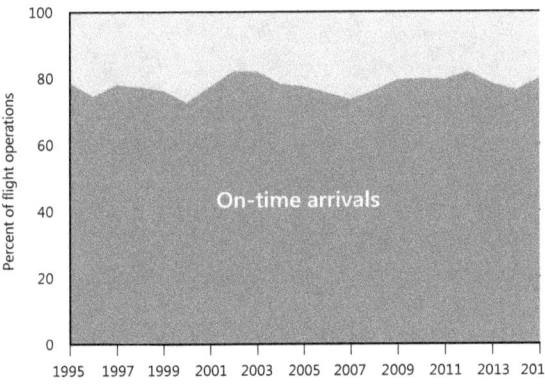

Note: Flights arriving at the gate within 15 minutes of scheduled arrival time are on time.

Source: U.S. Department of Transportation, Bureau of Transportation Statistics, Office of Airline Information, available at www.bts.gov as of October 2016.

5-4   U.S. Airport Delays by Cause: 2015
percent of delayed time

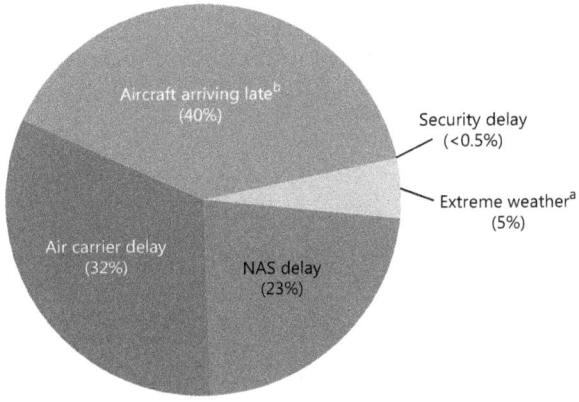

[a]Includes weather events that prevent flying. Other weather delays that slow operations are included under other categories. [b]Delay resulting from a previous flight with the same aircraft arriving late.

Key: NAS = Delays attributable to the national aviation system (NAS) that refer to a broad set of conditions, such as nonextreme weather, airport operations, heavy traffic volume, and air traffic control.

Note: Percents do not add to 100 due to rounding.

Source: U.S. Department of Transportation, Bureau of Transportation Statistics, Office of Airline Information, available at www.bts.gov as of October 2016.

5-5 U.S. Major Airport Performance Rankings: 2015
by percent of on-time arrivals

	Airport	Percent
Top 5	Salt Lake City, UT	86.9
	Atlanta, GA	84.4
	Portland, OR	83.9
	Charlotte, NC	83.4
	Seattle, WA	83.2
	All major U.S. airports	81.7
Bottom 5	Chicago, IL (ORD)	77.0
	San Francisco, CA	76.7
	New York, NY (JFK)	76.4
	Newark, NJ	75.4
	New York, NY (LGA)	70.9

Note: Flights arriving at the gate within 15 minutes of scheduled arrival time are on time.

Source: U.S. Department of Transportation, Bureau of Transportation Statistics, Office of Airline Information, available at www.bts.gov as of October 2016.

5-6 Amtrak On-Time Performance: FY1990–FY2015

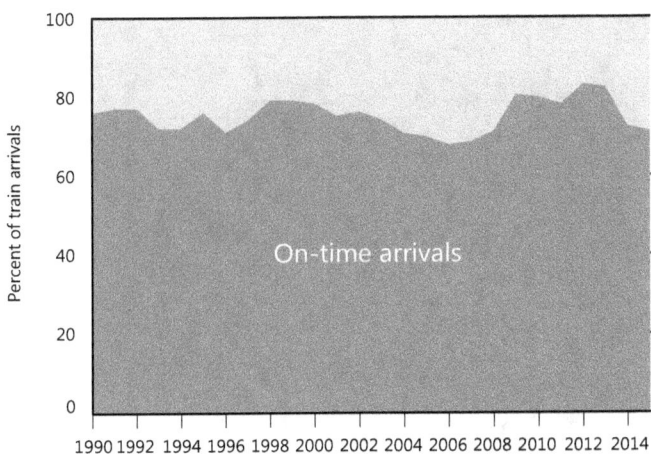

Note: On-time performance is a percentage measure of train performance. A train is considered on time if it arrives at the final destination, or end-point, within an allowed number of minutes, or tolerance, of its scheduled arrival time. Trains are allowed a certain tolerance at the end-point based on the number of miles traveled:

Trip length	On-time tolerance
0-250 miles	10 minutes
251-350 miles	15 minutes
351-450 miles	20 minutes
451-550 miles	25 minutes
>551 miles	30 minutes

Source: As cited in U.S. Department of Transportation, Bureau of Transportation Statistics, *National Transportation Statistics*, table 1-73, available at www.bts.gov as of October 2016.

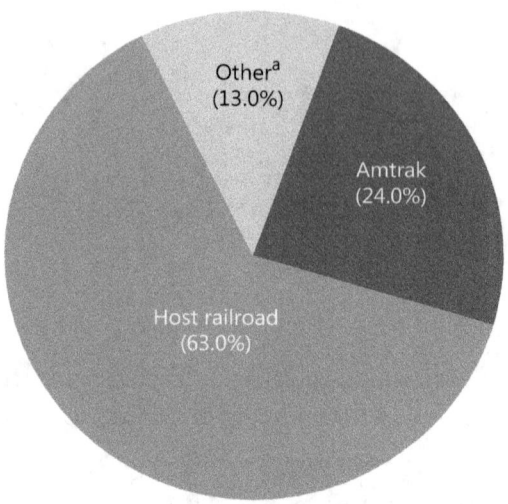

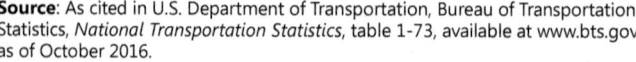

[a] Delays not attributable to Amtrak or other host railroads, such as customs and immigration, law enforcement action, weather, or waiting for scheduled departure time.

Source: As cited in U.S. Department of Transportation, Bureau of Transportation Statistics, *National Transportation Statistics*, table 1-73, available at www.bts.gov as of October 2016.

6   ECONOMY

Transportation is a major sector of the U.S. economy. The transportation system moves people and goods, employs millions of workers, generates revenue, and consumes resources and services provided by other sectors.

6-1   U.S. GDP by Spending Category: 2015
percent of GDP

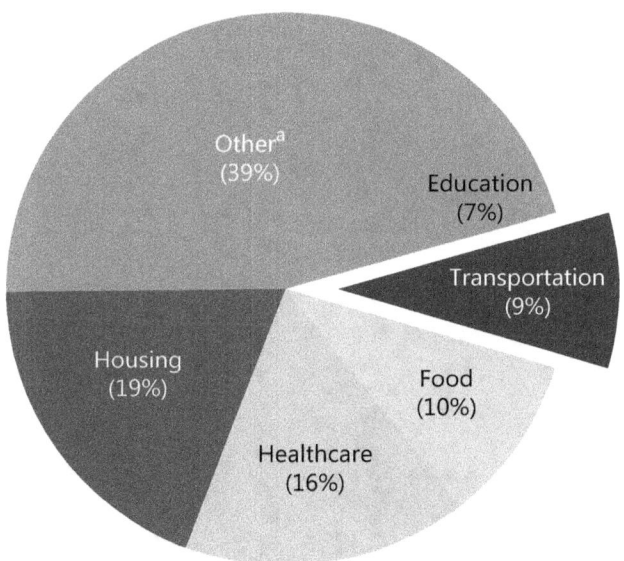

Other[a]
(39%)

Education
(7%)

Transportation
(9%)

Housing
(19%)

Food
(10%)

Healthcare
(16%)

[a]Includes all other categories (e.g., entertainment, personal care products and services, and payments to pension plans).

Source: As cited in U.S. Department of Transportation, Bureau of Transportation Statistics, *National Transportation Statistics*, table 3-9, available at www.bts.gov as of October 2016.

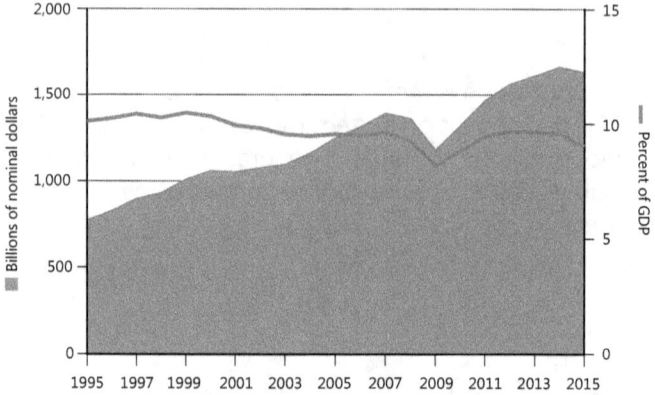

Source: as cited in U.S. Department of Transportation, Bureau of Transportation Statistics, *National Transportation Statistics*, table 3-9, available at www. bts.gov as of October 2016.

6-3 Transportation-Related Final Demand

billions of chained 2009 dollars

Category	2005	2015
Personal consumption of transportation	**1,008**	**1,021**
Motor vehicles and parts	400	419
Motor vehicle fuels, lubricants, and fluids	273	267
Transportation services	335	335
Gross private domestic investment	**206**	**314**
Transportation structures	8	12
Transportation equipment	198	302
Government transportation-related purchases	**297**	**U**
Federal purchases	33	U
State and local purchases	246	U
Defense-related purchases	18	U
Exports (+)	**226**	**321**
Imports (-)	**359**	**467**
Total transportation-related final demand	**1,374**	**1,196**
U.S. GDP	**14,234**	**16,397**

Key: U = unavailable.

Notes: Data may not add to totals due to rounding. Transportation-related final demand measures the size of transportation functions in relation to the GDP. It includes the transportation portion of the four components of the GDP: personal consumption, gross private domestic investment, government purchases, and net exports of goods and services.

Source: As cited in U.S. Department of Transportation, Bureau of Transportation Statistics, *National Transportation Statistics*, table 3-4, available at www.bts. gov as of October 2016.

6-4   Household Expenses by Category: 2015
percent of average annual household expenses

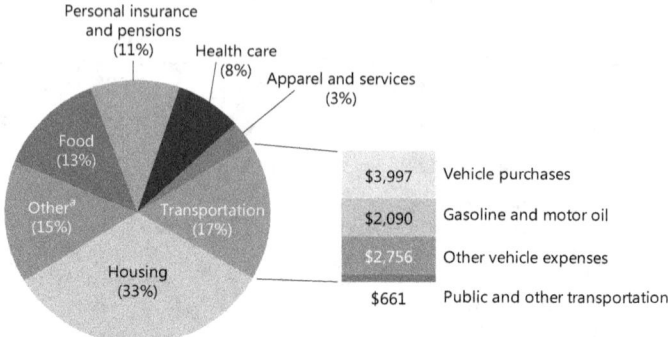

Personal insurance
and pensions
(11%)   Health care
(8%)   Apparel and services
(3%)

Food
(13%)

Other^a
(15%)

Transportation
(17%)

Housing
(33%)

$3,997	Vehicle purchases
$2,090	Gasoline and motor oil
$2,756	Other vehicle expenses
$661	Public and other transportation

^a Includes alcoholic beverages, cash contributions, education, entertainment, personal care products and services, reading, tobacco products and smoking supplies, and other miscellaneous items.

Source: U.S. Department of Labor, Bureau of Labor Statistics, *Consumer Expenditure Survey*, available at www.bls.gov/cex as of October 2016.

6-5   Household Transportation Expenses: 1985–2015

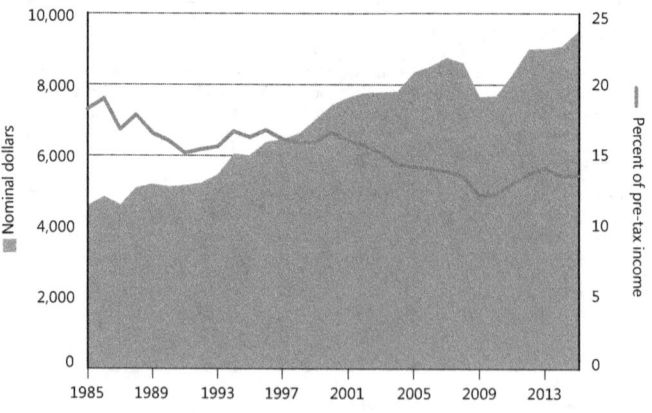

Source: U.S. Department of Labor, Bureau of Labor Statistics, *Consumer Expenditure Survey*, available at www.bls.gov/cex as of October 2016.

chain-type index: 2000 = 100, seasonally adjusted

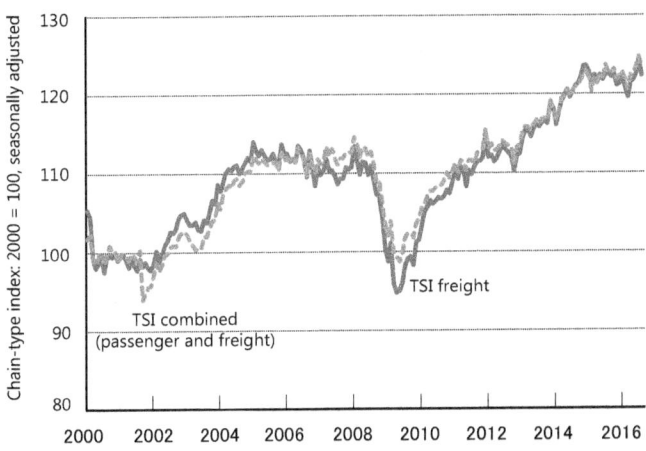

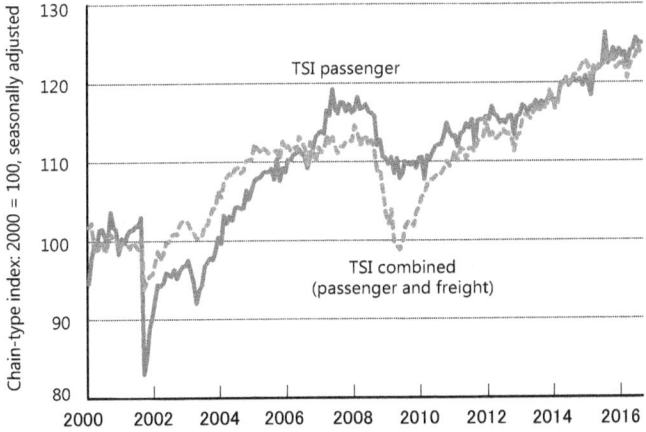

Notes: The TSI, created by the U.S. Department of Transportation, Bureau of Transportation Statistics, is a measure of the month-to month changes in the output of services provided by the for-hire transportation industries. TSI data change monthly due to the use of concurrent seasonal analysis, which results in seasonal analysis factors changing as each month's data are added.

Source: U.S. Department of Transportation, Bureau of Transportation Statistics, available at www.bts.gov as of October 2016.

6-7 Employment in Transportation-Related Industries

thousands

Category	2005	2015
For-hire transportation and warehousing	**4,361**	**4,845**
Air	501	444
Rail	228	242
Water	61	65
Truck	1,398	1,455
Transit and ground passenger	389	475
Pipeline	38	49
Scenic and sightseeing	29	32
Support activities	552	649
Couriers and messengers	571	608
Warehousing and storage	595	813
Transportation-related manufacturing[a]	**2,130**	**1,891**
Other transportation-related industries	**5,203**	**5,334**
Postal service	**774**	**597**
Government employment[b]	**888**	**U**
Total transportation-related labor force	**13,395**	**12,710**
U.S. labor force	**134,051**	**141,865**

[a]Includes transportation equipment; petroleum products; tires; rubber; plastics; search, detection, navigation, guidance, aeronautical, and nautical systems; and instrument manufacturing. [b]Fiscal year data for federal, state, and local personnel. U=data are unavailable.

Notes: Annual averages based on NAICS data. Details may not add to totals due to rounding.

Source: As cited in U.S. Department of Transportation, Bureau of Transportation Statistics, *National Transportation Statistics*, table 3-23, available at www.bts.gov as of October 2016.

6-8 Motor Vehicle Gasoline Prices: Jan. 1980 – Aug. 2016

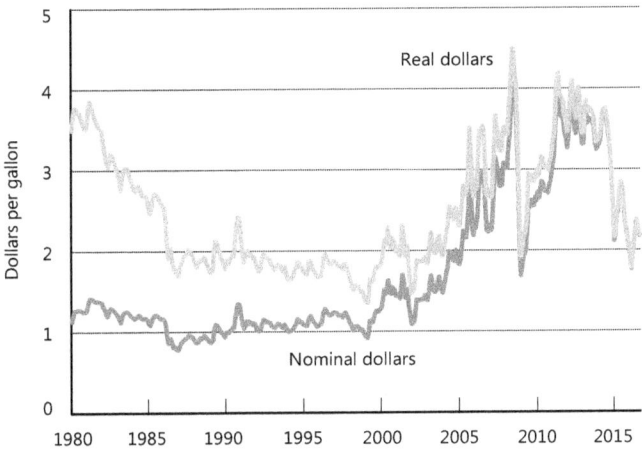

Notes: Nominal prices are average monthly prices of regular grade motor vehicle gasoline. Real prices are in October 2016 dollars adjusted by the Consumer Price Index (1982–84=1).

Source: U.S. Department of Energy, Energy Information Administration, *Short-Term Energy Outlook*, available at www.eia.doe.gov as of October 2016.

7 ENVIRONMENT

The U.S. transportation system is a major consumer of energy and generates environmental impacts.

7-1   Energy Consumption by Sector: 1960–2015

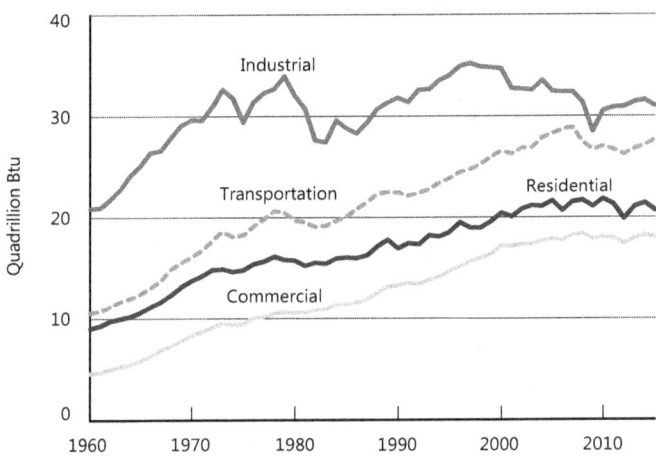

Key: Btu = British thermal unit.

Note: Includes primary energy consumption, electricity retail sales, and electrical system energy losses.

Source: U.S. Department of Energy, U.S. Energy Information Administration, *Monthly Energy Review*, available at www.eia.gov/totalenergy/data/monthly as of October 2016.

7-2 Transportation Energy Consumption by Source: 2015
percent of Btu consumed

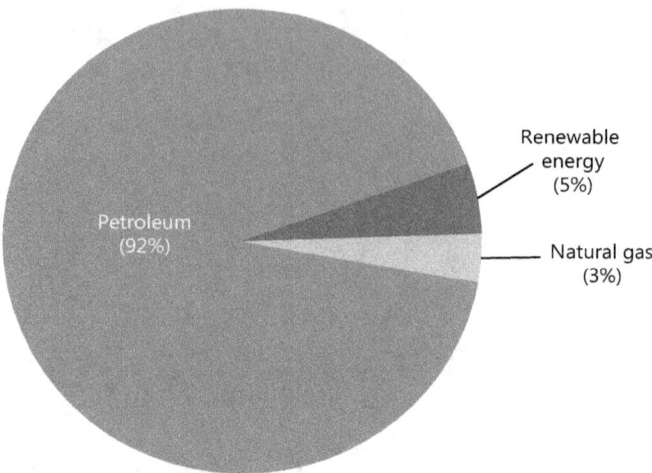

Petroleum (92%)

Renewable energy (5%)

Natural gas (3%)

Key: Btu = British thermal unit.

Notes: Includes primary energy consumed. Excludes electricity retail sales and electrical system energy losses.

Source: U.S. Department of Energy, U.S. Energy Information Administration, *Monthly Energy Review*, available at www.eia.gov/totalenergy/data/monthly as of October 2016.

7-3 Petroleum Consumption by Sector: 1960–2015

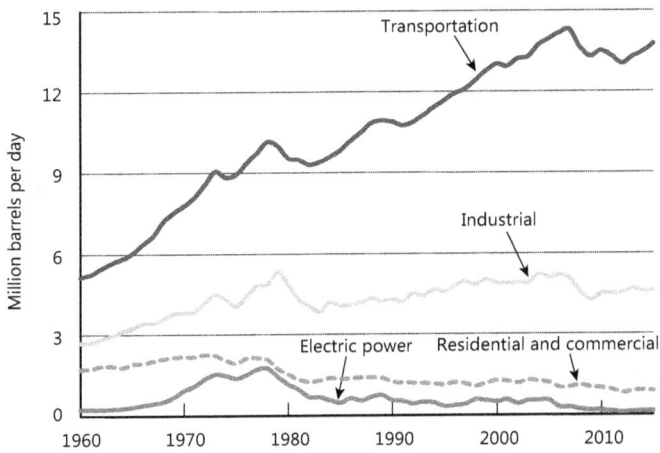

Source: U.S. Department of Energy, U.S. Energy Information Administration, *Monthly Energy Review*, available at www.eia.gov/totalenergy/data/monthly as of October 2016.

7-4 Greenhouse Gas Emissions by Sector: 1990–2014

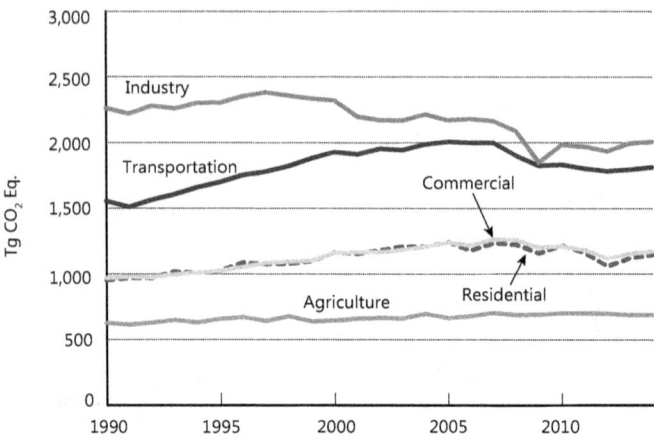

Key: Tg CO_2 Eq. = teragrams of carbon dioxide equivalent. A teragram = 1 million metric tons.

Notes: Electric power sector emissions are distributed across sectors. Emissions include CO_2, CH_4, N_2O, HFCs, PFCs, and SF_6.

Source: U.S. Environmental Protection Agency, *Inventory of U.S. Greenhouse Gas Emissions and Sinks: 1990–2014 Report Tables*, available at www.epa.gov/climatechange/ghgemissions/usinventoryreport.html as of October 2016.

7-5 Greenhouse Gas Emissions by Transportation Mode: 2014

Percent of Tg CO$_2$ Eq.

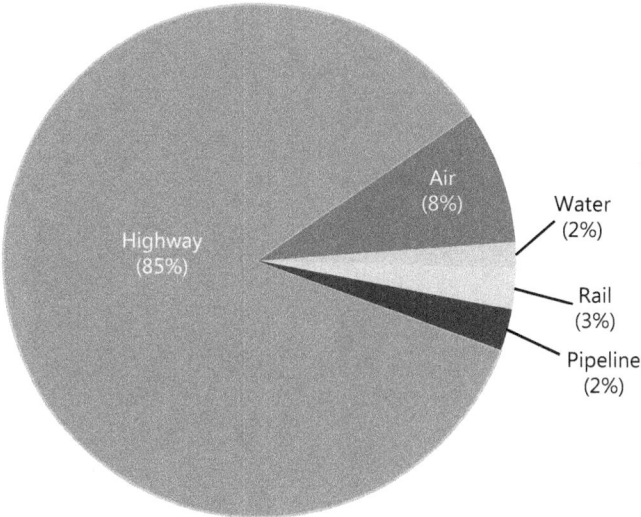

Key: Tg CO$_2$ Eq. = teragrams of carbon dioxide equivalent. A teragram = 1 million metric tons.

Notes: Percents may not add to 100 due to rounding. Does not include International Bunker Fuels.

Source: U.S. Environmental Protection Agency, *Inventory of U.S. Greenhouse Gas Emissions and Sinks: 1990–2014 Report Tables*, available at www.epa.gov/climatechange/ghgemissions/usinventoryreport.html as of October 2016.

7-6 Highway Vehicle Air Pollutant Emissions: 2002–2014

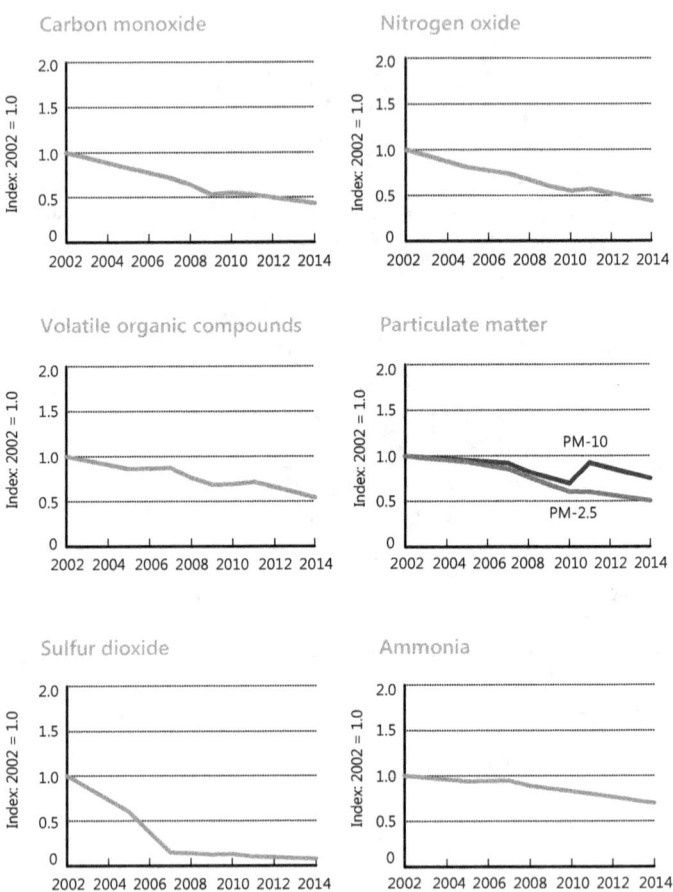

Carbon monoxide

Nitrogen oxide

Volatile organic compounds

Particulate matter

PM-10

PM-2.5

Sulfur dioxide

Ammonia

Key: PM-10 = airborne particulates of less than 10 microns; PM-2.5 = airborne particulates of less than 2.5 microns.

Notes: Indices are calculated using data on highway vehicle emissions only. Particulate matters include PM without condensibles.

Sources: As cited in U.S. Department of Transportation, Bureau of Transportation Statistics, *National Transportation Statistics*, tables 4-45 through 4-50, available at www.bts.gov as of October 2016.

7-7 Fuel Economy of Light-Duty Vehicles: 1990–2014

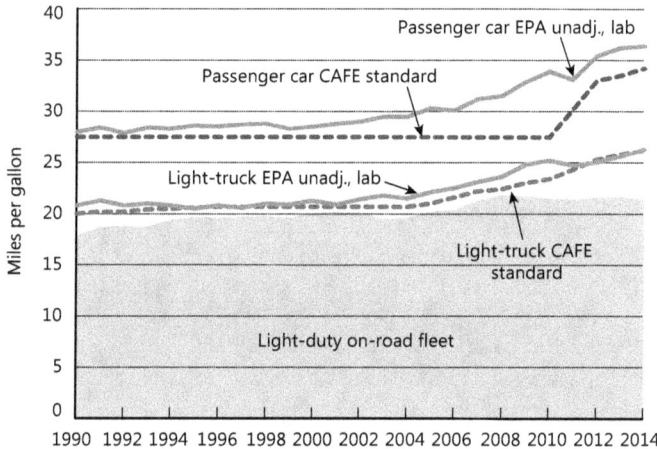

Key: CAFE = Corporate Average Fuel Economy

Notes: New fleet data and CAFE standards are for vehicle model years. On-road fleet data include passenger cars and light trucks and are estimated using average miles traveled per gallon of fuel consumed for each calendar year.

Source: As cited in U.S. Department of Transportation, Bureau of Transportation Statistics, *National Transportation Statistics*, table 4-23, available at www.bts.gov as of October 2016.

7-8 Alternative Fuel Vehicles by Fuel Type: 2004–2014

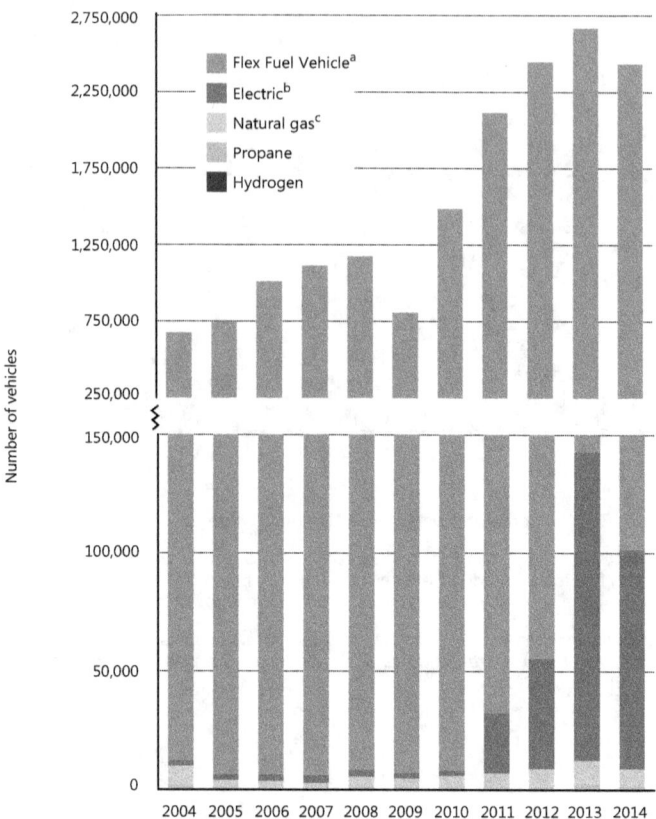

[a]Flex fuel/ethanol vehicles are capable of running on E85, plain gasoline, or any ethanol-gasoline blends in between. [b]Excludes gasoline-electric hybrids. [c]Includes compressed natural gas (CNG) and liquified natural gas (LNG).

Note: Includes the total number of light, medium, and heavy duty vehicles that were manufactured or converted by vehicle suppliers (companies or organizations) in the associated calendar year.

Source: U.S. Department of Energy, Energy Information Administration, Alternative Fuel Vehicle Data, Supplier Database, available at www.eia.gov/renewable/afv/ as of October 2016.

7-9 Gasoline Hybrid and Electric Vehicle Sales: 2000–2015

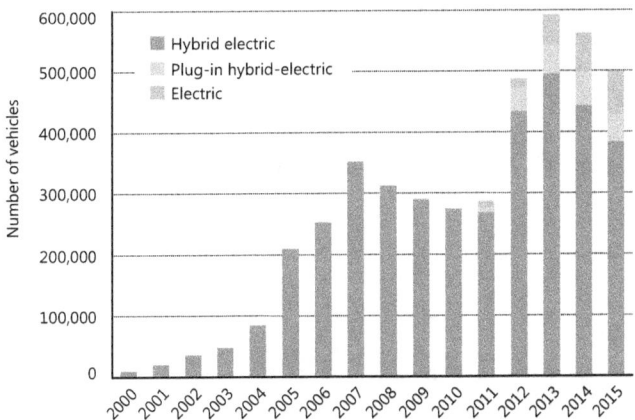

Notes: Includes the new sales of light duty gasoline vehicles including hybrid-electric vehicles (HEV), plug-in hybrid-electric vehicles (PHEV), and electric vehicles (EV). Plug-in hybrid electric vehicles include plug-in hybrid and extended range EVs but do not include neighborhood electric vehicles, low speed electric vehicles, or two-wheeled electric vehicles. A hybrid electric vehicle is a vehicle powered by a combination of battery-electric motor(s) and an internal combustion engine.

Source: U.S. Department of Energy, Energy Information Administration, Alternative Fuels Data Center, available at www.bts.gov.as of October 2016.

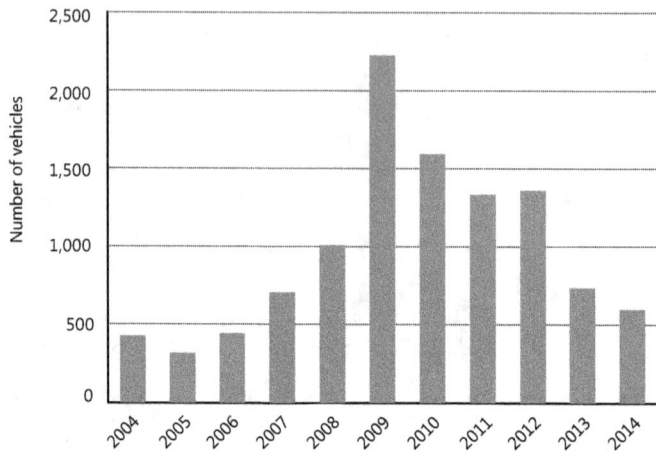

Note: Includes the total number of vehicles that were manufactured or converted by vehicle suppliers (companies or organizations) in the associated calendar year.

Source: U.S. Department of Energy, Energy Information Administration, Alternative Fuel Vehicle Data, Supplier Database, available at www.eia.gov/renewable/afv/ as of October 2016.

GLOSSARY

Air carrier: Certificated provider of scheduled and nonscheduled services.

Alternative fueled vehicle: A vehicle designed to operate on an alternative fuel (e.g., compressed natural gas, propane, electricity). The vehicle can be either a dedicated vehicle designed to operate exclusively on alternative fuel or a non-dedicated vehicle designed to operate on alternative fuel and/or traditional fuel.

Chained dollars: A method of adjusting to real dollar amounts to account for both changes in price-levels and the composition of output over time. This is completed by using a chain-weighted type index, or average weights in successive time periods, to get a comparable time series of data.

Class I railroad: Railroads earning adjusted annual operating revenues for three consecutive years of $250,000,000 or more, based on 1991 dollars with an adjustment factor applied to subsequent years.

Commuter rail: Urban/suburban passenger train service for short-distance travel between a central city and adjacent suburbs run on tracks of a traditional railroad system. Does not include heavy or light rail transit service.

Demand response transit: A nonfixed-route, nonfixed-schedule form of transportation that operates in response to calls from passengers or their agents to the transit operator or dispatcher.

Directional route-miles: The sum of the mileage in each direction over which transit vehicles travel while in revenue service.

Enplanements: Total number of revenue passengers boarding aircraft.

For-hire: Refers to a vehicle operated on behalf of or by a company that provides services to external customers for a fee. It is distinguished from private transportation services, in which a firm transports its own freight and does not offer its transportation services to other shippers.

General aviation: Civil aviation operations other than those air carriers holding a Certificate of Public Convenience and Necessity. Types of aircraft used in general aviation range from corporate, multi-engine jets piloted by a professional crew to amateur-built, single-engine, piston-driven, acrobatic planes.

Gross Domestic Product: The total value of goods and services produced by labor and property located in the United States. As long as the labor and property are located in the United States, the suppliers may be either U.S. residents or residents of foreign countries.

Heavy-rail transit: High-speed transit rail operated on rights-of-way that exclude all other vehicles and pedestrians.

Hybrid electric vehicle: Hybrid electric vehicles combine features of internal combustion engines and electric motors. Unlike 100% electric vehicles, hybrid vehicles do not need to be plugged into an external source of electricity to be recharged. Most hybrid vehicles operate on gasoline.

International Roughness Index (IRI): A scale for pavement roughness based on the simulated response of a generic motor vehicle to the roughness in a single wheel path of the road surface.

Lane-miles: One mile of one lane of road.

Light duty vehicle: Includes passenger cars, light trucks, vans, pickup trucks, and sport/utility vehicles regardless of wheelbase.

Light-rail transit: Urban transit rail operated on a reserved right-of-way that may be crossed by roads used by motor vehicles and pedestrians.

Nominal dollars: A market value that does not take inflation into account and reflects prices and quantities that is current during the period being measured.

Nonself-propelled vessels: Includes dry cargo, tank barges, and railroad car floats that operate in U.S. ports and waterways.

Oceangoing vessels: Includes U.S. flag, privately-owned merchant fleet of oceangoing, self-propelled, cargo-carrying vessels of 1,000 gross tons or greater.

Particulates: Carbon particles formed by partial oxidation and reduction of hydrocarbon fuel. Also included are trace quantities of metal oxides and nitrides originating from engine wear, component degradation, and inorganic fuel additives.

Passenger-mile: One passenger transported one mile. For example, one vehicle traveling 3 miles carrying 5 passengers generates 15 passenger miles.

Personal communication: Involves contacting the source for data if not publicly available.

Plug-in hybrid electric vehicles: Plug-in hybrids use the electric battery as the primary energy source by relying on battery power for propulsion for a limited range (15-40 miles) before switching to internal combustion propulsion (thus reducing gasoline consumption).

Reliever airports: Airports designated by the Federal Aviation Administration to relieve congestion at commercial service airports and to provide improved general aviation access to the overall community.

Seasonally adjusted: Measures the real differences in data trends by adjusting for seasonal factors such as the change in the number of days, weekends, holidays, or other seasonal activity in a month such as vacation travel.

Self-propelled vessels: Includes dry cargo vessels, tankers, and offshore supply vessels, tugboats, pushboats, and passenger vessels, such as excursion/sightseeing boats, combination passenger and dry cargo vessels, and ferries.

Short ton: A unit of weight equal to 2,000 pounds.

Structurally deficient: Structural deficiencies are characterized by deteriorated conditions of significant bridge elements and reduced load-carrying capacity.

Real Dollars: A method of adjusting nominal dollars to account for price level changes over time. It reflects purchasing power in a given period.

Tg CO2 Eq.: Teragrams of carbon dioxide equivalent, a metric measure used to compare the emissions from various greenhouse gases based on their global warming potential.

Ton-mile: A unit of measure equal to movement of one ton over one mile.

Transportation Services Index: BTS' monthly measure indicating the relative change in the volume of services over time performed by the for-hire transportation sector. Change is shown relative to a base year, which is given a value of 100. The TSI covers the activities of for-hire freight carriers, for-hire passenger carriers, and a combination of the two. See www.bts.gov for a detailed explanation.

Transportation Services Index Combined: The combined Transportation Services Index (TSI) includes available data on freight traffic, as well as passenger travel, that have been weighted to yield a monthly measure of transportation services output.

Transportation Services Index Freight: The freight TSI measures the output of the for-hire freight transportation industry and consists of data from for-hire trucking, rail, inland waterways, pipelines and air freight.

Transportation Services Index Passenger: The passenger TSI includes local transit, intercity passenger rail, and passenger air transportation, that have been weighted to yield a monthly measure of transportation services output.

Unlinked passenger trip: The number of passengers who board public transportation vehicles. Passengers are counted each time they board vehicles no matter how many vehicles they use to travel from their origin to their destination.

Vehicle-mile: One vehicle traveling one mile.

Statistics published in this Pocket Guide to Transportation come from many different sources. Some statistics are based on samples and are subject to sampling variability. Statistics may also be subject to omissions and errors in reporting, recording, and processing.

Photo Credits

Cover (left to right)
   Marcelo da Mota Silva
   BTS Stock Photo
   Alpha Wingfield
   Alpha Wingfield
   BTS Stock Photo
   Steven P. Gass

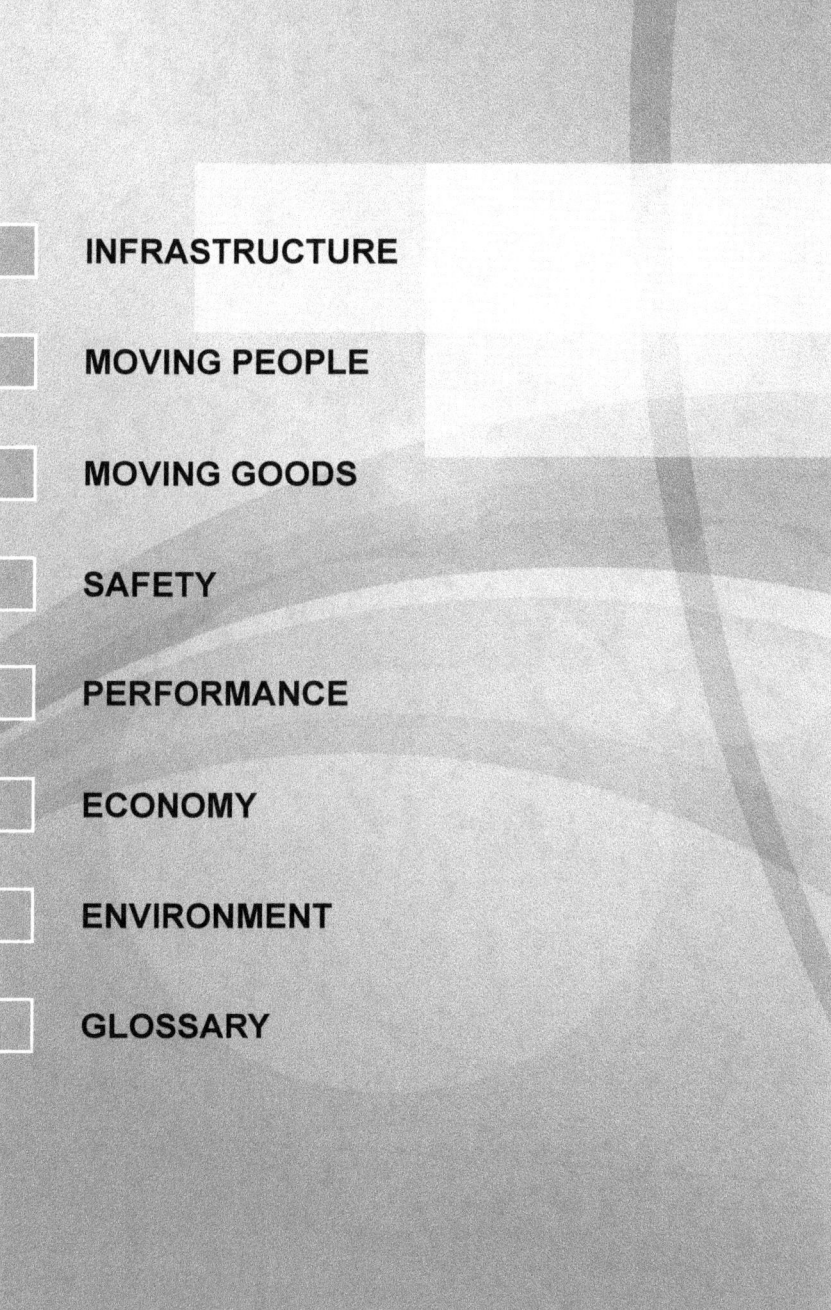